Dehydrating Food - Dehydrating For Backpacking And Camping

DANA MCCARTHY

Published by Nimzo Media, 2024.

DEHYDRATING FOOD - DEHYDRATING FOR BACKPACKING AND CAMPING

First edition. February 18, 2024.

Copyright © 2024 DANA MCCARTHY.

ISBN: 979-8224587278

Written by DANA MCCARTHY.

Also by DANA MCCARTHY

Beginners Guide To Dehydrating Food
Dehydrating Food - Dehydrating For Backpacking And Camping

Dehydrating food - Dehydrating for Backpacking and Camping

Table of Contents

10 Chapter 10: Smarter Packing for Backpacking and Camping

11 Chapter 11: Flavor Enhancements and Seasonings

12 Chapter 12: Dehydrating Fruits and Vegetables

13 Chapter 13: DIY Dehydrated Meal Kits

14 Chapter 14: Hydration for Backpacking and Camping

3 Incorporating hydration into meal planning for outdoor adventures

15 Chapter 15: Advanced Dehydrating Techniques

1 Exploring complex recipes and meal ideas for experienced campers

2 Innovative dehydrating methods for unique and gourmet outdoor meals

Chapter 1: The Basics of Dehydrating

Understanding the benefits of dehydrating for backpacking and camping

Throughout my years of backpacking and camping, I have come to appreciate the art of dehydrating food. It is an essential skill that every outdoor enthusiast should learn. Dehydrating food allows you to create mouthwatering meals that are perfect for the outdoors, while also preserving food without sacrificing flavor. In this subchapter, I will share with you the benefits of dehydrating for backpacking and camping, as well as some effective techniques and tips to make your meals both nutritious and delicious. So, let's get started!

When it comes to outdoor adventures, weight and space are always a concern. Carrying heavy and bulky food is not only tiresome but can also limit the amount of gear you can bring along. This is where dehydrated meals truly shine. They are incredibly lightweight and space-saving, allowing you to carry more food without sacrificing valuable backpack space. Plus, with the right techniques, you can still enjoy meals that are packed with nutrients and full of flavor. In this subchapter, I will show you how to master the art of meal planning for extended adventures and unlock the secrets to rehydrating meals for a satisfying dining experience.

One of the key benefits of dehydrating food for backpacking and camping is that it allows you to save weight and space in your backpack without compromising on nutrition. Traditional meals often contain a lot of water content, which adds unnecessary weight. By dehydrating your food, you remove the water and significantly reduce the weight of your meals. This means you can carry more food without overburdening yourself. In addition, dehydrated meals take up minimal space in your backpack, giving you more room for other essential items. So, if you're looking to go on longer adventures or simply want to lighten your load, dehydrating food is the way to go.

Another advantage of dehydrated meals is that they can be easily rehydrated, allowing you to enjoy a hot and satisfying meal after a long day of outdoor activities. Whether you're on a multi-day backpacking trip or camping out in the wilderness, having a warm meal at the end of the day can be a real morale booster. With the right techniques, you can rehydrate your dehydrated meals to perfection, ensuring that they are not only edible but also delicious. In this subchapter, I will share some tips and tricks for rehydrating your meals to create a dining experience that rivals even the best restaurant meals.

Essential equipment for dehydrating food

When it comes to dehydrating food for backpacking and camping, having the right equipment is essential. In this section, we will explore the essential tools and accessories that will help you master the art of food dehydration. By using the right equipment, you can preserve food without sacrificing flavor and create delicious meals that are perfect for the outdoors.

The first and most important tool for dehydrating food is a dehydrator. When choosing a dehydrator for backpacking and camping, there are a few key factors to consider. Look for a dehydrator that is compact and lightweight, as this will make it easier to transport on your adventures. Additionally, make sure the dehydrator has adjustable temperature settings, as different foods require different drying temperatures. This will give you more control over the dehydration process and ensure that your food is dried thoroughly and evenly.

Another essential tool for dehydrating food is a mandoline slicer. This handy device will make it much easier to slice fruits, vegetables, and other ingredients uniformly, ensuring that they dry at the same rate. Look for a mandoline slicer that is lightweight and compact, so it won't take up too much space in your backpack. Additionally, choose a slicer with adjustable thickness settings, so you can create thin slices for faster drying or thicker slices for a chewier texture.

A vacuum sealer is another valuable tool for preserving dehydrated food. By removing the air from the packaging, a vacuum sealer helps to extend the shelf life of your dehydrated meals. Look for a compact and lightweight vacuum sealer that is easy to use in the field. Additionally, choose one that is compatible with reusable bags, as this will make it more environmentally friendly and cost-effective.

To store your dehydrated food, you will need suitable containers. Mason jars are a great option, as they are durable, airtight, and can be reused. They are perfect for storing dehydrated fruits, vegetables, and spices. Mylar bags are another excellent choice, especially for longer backpacking trips. These bags are lightweight, durable, and provide an excellent barrier against moisture and oxygen, keeping your food fresh and protected.

Lastly, consider investing in mesh screens and fruit leather trays for your dehydrator. Mesh screens are designed to prevent smaller food items or ingredients from falling through the trays, ensuring that everything dries evenly. Fruit leather trays are perfect for making homemade fruit roll-ups and are a fun and delicious snack option for the trail. These accessories will enhance your dehydrating experience and open up a world of creative possibilities.

Tips for selecting the best foods to dehydrate

When it comes to dehydrating food for your backpacking and camping adventures, selecting the right foods is key. Not only do you want to consider the taste and texture of the food once it's been dehydrated, but you also need to think about the nutritional value and cooking time. In this subchapter, I'll be sharing some tips to help you choose the best foods to dehydrate.

1. Start by considering taste and texture:

When dehydrating food, it's important to choose foods that will still taste great and have a pleasant texture once rehydrated. Some foods that work well for dehydration include fruits like apples, bananas, and strawberries, as well as vegetables like bell peppers, carrots, and mushrooms. These foods retain their flavors and textures after the dehydration process.

2. Don't forget about nutritional value:

While it's important for your dehydrated meals to taste delicious, you also want them to provide the necessary nutrients for your outdoor adventures. Consider selecting foods that are rich in vitamins and minerals, like kale, spinach, and sweet potatoes. These nutritious foods will help keep you energized and healthy during your backpacking trips.

3. Cooking time matters:

Another factor to consider when choosing foods to dehydrate is the cooking time. Some foods take longer to dehydrate than others, so it's important to plan accordingly. If you're short on time, opt for foods that dehydrate quickly, such as thin slices of citrus fruits or small pieces of lean meat. These will save you time and ensure that your dehydrated meals are ready when you need them.

By considering taste, texture, nutritional value, and cooking time, you'll be able to select the best foods to dehydrate for your backpacking and camping trips. Get creative with your choices and don't be afraid to try new combinations. Remember, dehydrating food is a skill that takes practice, so keep experimenting and refining your techniques.

Chapter 2: Dehydrating Techniques

Slicing and preparing foods for dehydration

I'm thrilled that you are ready to dive into the world of dehydrating foods for your backpacking and camping adventures. In this subchapter, we will cover the proper techniques for slicing and preparing foods for dehydration.

When it comes to dehydrating fruits, vegetables, and meats, it's essential to follow the right techniques to ensure successful results. Here are some tips to get you started:

Firstly, make sure to choose ripe and fresh produce for dehydration. This will guarantee that your dehydrated snacks are packed with flavor.

When slicing fruits and vegetables, it's important to cut them into thin and even pieces. This allows for better airflow and even dehydration. A mandoline slicer or a sharp knife can be your best friends for achieving consistent slices.

For meats, it's crucial to trim off any excess fat before slicing. Fat can hinder the dehydration process and affect the overall quality of the final product. Aim for thin strips to facilitate the drying process.

Another important aspect of preparing foods for dehydration is blanching. This process involves briefly boiling vegetables in salted water, and then quickly submerging them in ice water to stop the cooking process. Blanching helps to preserve color, texture, and nutrients in the final dehydrated product.

After slicing and blanching, it's time to arrange your food on the dehydrator trays. Make sure to leave enough space between the slices or pieces to allow for proper airflow throughout the dehydration process.

Lastly, it's crucial to monitor the temperature and time required for dehydration. Different foods have different drying times, so it's essential to consult a reliable drying guide or follow the manufacturer's instructions for your specific dehydrator model.

By following these techniques, you will be well on your way to mastering the art of dehydrating foods for your outdoor adventures. Get ready to enjoy delicious and nutritious meals on your backpacking trips!

Using a dehydrator for optimal results

When it comes to using a dehydrator for optimal results, there are a few key things to keep in mind. Let me guide you through the process to ensure that you get the most out of your dehydrator and achieve perfectly dried foods every time.

Step 1: Prepare your food

Before using your dehydrator, it's important to properly prepare your food. This may involve washing fruits and vegetables, trimming fat off of meats, or slicing larger items into smaller pieces. By taking the time to prep your food correctly, you'll ensure that it dries evenly and efficiently.

Step 2: Arrange your food

Next, it's time to arrange your food on the dehydrator trays. Make sure to leave enough space between items to allow for proper airflow. This will help to ensure even drying and prevent any sticking or clumping.

Step 3: Set the temperature and time

Now it's time to set the temperature and time on your dehydrator. Different foods require different settings, so refer to the user manual or do a quick online search for the optimal temperature and time for the specific food you're drying. This will help to preserve the flavors and nutrients of your food while achieving the desired level of dehydration.

Step 4: Monitor the process

While your food is drying, it's important to keep an eye on the process. Check the trays periodically to ensure that everything is drying evenly and adjust the temperature or time if necessary. This will help prevent any over-drying or under-drying of your food.

Step 5: Store your dried food

Once your food is fully dehydrated, it's time to store it properly. Make sure to use airtight containers or vacuum-sealed bags to keep your food fresh and free from moisture. Store your dried food in a cool, dark place to ensure maximum shelf life.

By following these steps and paying attention to the details, you'll be able to use your dehydrator for optimal results. Enjoy the convenience and deliciousness of dehydrated food on your outdoor adventures!

Alternative methods for dehydrating without a dehydrator

Now that we've explored different options for dehydrating food, let's dive into some alternative methods for dehydrating without a dehydrator. These methods are perfect for backpacking and camping trips, allowing you to create delicious meals that are lightweight and easy to pack.

One method you can try is oven drying. This involves using your regular oven to dehydrate food. Start by slicing your fruits, vegetables, or meats into thin, uniform pieces. Place them on a baking sheet or parchment paper, making sure to leave enough space between each piece for proper airflow. Set your oven to its lowest temperature, usually between 140°F (60°C) and 170°F (77°C), and leave the door slightly ajar to allow moisture to escape. It's important to keep a close eye on the food to ensure it doesn't burn or become overly dried. The drying process can take anywhere from a few hours to overnight, depending on the type and thickness of the food.

If you prefer a more natural approach, sun drying is an excellent option. This method requires ample sunlight and warm weather. Choose a sunny location with good air circulation and lay your food out on a mesh or wire rack. Make sure to cover the food with a lightweight fabric, such as cheesecloth, to protect it from insects and debris. Place the rack in a sunny spot, preferably elevated off the ground to promote air circulation. Leave the food to dry for several days, flipping it occasionally to ensure even drying. Sun drying may take longer than other methods, but it provides a truly natural and hands-off experience.

Another alternative method is air drying. This technique is ideal for herbs, flowers, and some fruits. Simply gather your ingredients in small bunches and hang them upside down in a well-ventilated area. Make sure to choose a space away from direct sunlight and moisture. Allow the food to dry for several days, or until it is completely dried and crumbly to the touch. Air drying is a simple and effective way to preserve the flavors of your ingredients.

When using these alternative dehydration methods, there are a few tips to keep in mind for successful results. Firstly, always properly prepare your food by washing, peeling, and removing any seeds or pits. This will ensure optimal flavor and texture. Secondly, slice your ingredients into uniform sizes to promote even drying. This will also help reduce drying time. Lastly, store your dehydrated food in airtight containers or vacuum-sealed bags to maintain freshness and prolong shelf life.

With these alternative methods, you can unlock the secrets to preserving and dehydrating food without the need for a dehydrator. Feel free to experiment with different ingredients and seasoning combinations to create mouthwatering meals that are perfect for the outdoors. Happy dehydrating!

Chapter 3: Mouthwatering Meal Ideas

Recipes for dehydrated breakfasts

Now that we've covered the basics of dehydrating breakfast meals, it's time to dive into some mouthwatering recipes that are perfect for enjoying in the great outdoors. These recipes are not only delicious but also lightweight and easy to prepare, making them ideal for backpacking and camping adventures.

This recipe is a classic for a reason. Oatmeal is a hearty and nutritious breakfast option that provides sustained energy throughout the day. To dehydrate oatmeal, simply cook your desired amount of oats with water or milk until they reach a thick and creamy consistency. Spread the cooked oatmeal onto a dehydrator tray and dry it at a low temperature until it becomes brittle. Once dehydrated, you can store it in a ziplock bag or airtight container. To enjoy, simply add hot water or milk to rehydrate the oatmeal and add any toppings you desire, such as dried fruits, nuts, or honey.

If you're looking for a grab-and-go breakfast option, these dehydrated breakfast bars are the perfect choice. To make these bars, mix together rolled oats, honey or maple syrup, nut butter of your choice, and any additional ingredients you prefer, such as dried fruits, chocolate chips or nuts. Press the mixture firmly into a baking dish lined with parchment paper and dehydrate it until it becomes firm and dry. Cut the bars into individual servings and store them in an airtight container. These bars are not only delicious but also packed with energy and nutrients, making them an excellent fuel source for your outdoor adventures.

Eggs are a breakfast staple, and this dehydrated egg scramble allows you to enjoy them even when you're on the go. To prepare this recipe, whisk together eggs, milk, and any desired seasonings, such as salt, pepper, and herbs. Pour the mixture onto a dehydrator tray and dry it until it becomes crisp and brittle. Once dehydrated, crumble the egg mixture into small pieces and store it in a ziplock bag or airtight container. To rehydrate the egg scramble, simply add hot water and let it sit for a few minutes until it becomes soft and fluffy. You can also add dehydrated vegetables, cheese, or bacon bits to enhance the flavor of the scramble.

With these dehydrated breakfast recipes, you can enjoy delicious and nutritious meals even when you're far from the comfort of your kitchen. Experiment with different flavors and ingredients to create your own personalized backpacking breakfast menu. Happy dehydrating!

Lunch and dinner options for the trail

When it comes to backpacking and camping, having delicious and nutritious meals is essential for keeping your energy levels up and your taste buds satisfied. In this section, we'll explore some fantastic dehydrated lunch and dinner options that are perfect for the trail.

Whether you're looking for a hearty pasta dish or a flavorful curry, dehydrating your meals allows you to carry lightweight and compact food without sacrificing taste. With a little bit of preparation and the right techniques, you can create mouthwatering meals that will make your outdoor adventures even more enjoyable.

Some popular dehydrated lunch and dinner options for the trail include:

- Dehydrated pasta dishes: From classic spaghetti and meatballs to creamy alfredo, you can dehydrate your favorite pasta dishes to enjoy on the trail. Just add hot water, and you'll have a satisfying meal in minutes.
- Dehydrated soups and stews: Warm and comforting, dehydrated soups and stews are perfect for chilly nights on the trail. Simply rehydrate them with hot water, and you'll have a delicious meal that will warm you from the inside out.

- Dehydrated curries and stir-fries: Add a touch of spice to your backpacking meals with dehydrated curries and stir-fries. Packed with flavor and nutrients, these meals are a great way to fuel your adventures.
- Dehydrated chili and beans: If you're craving something hearty and filling, dehydrated chili and beans are the way to go. Just rehydrate them, and you'll have a protein-packed meal that will keep you going all day long.

With these dehydrated options, you can save weight and space in your backpack without compromising on nutrition or taste. Plus, by mastering the art of meal planning for extended adventures, you can ensure that you have a variety of delicious meals to enjoy throughout your trip.

So, whether you're heading out for a weekend getaway or embarking on a longer expedition, be sure to experiment with dehydrated lunch and dinner recipes. Not only will you save time and effort on the trail, but you'll also have the satisfaction of enjoying a mouthwatering meal in the great outdoors.

Now that we've covered some tasty dehydrated meal options, let's move on to the next section, where we'll explore creative ideas for rehydrating and serving meals on the trail.

Delicious snacks and desserts for outdoor adventures

Now that you've learned the art of dehydrating for backpacking and camping, it's time to dive into creating some mouthwatering meals that are perfect for the outdoors. In this section, we'll explore some delicious snacks and desserts that will keep your energy levels up and satisfy your sweet tooth.

When you're out in the wilderness, it's important to have snacks that provide a boost of energy. Whether you're hiking up a steep trail or setting up camp for the night, these energy-boosting snacks will keep you fueled and ready for any adventure.

First up, we have trail mix. This classic snack is a staple for outdoor enthusiasts. You can create your own custom mix by combining nuts, dried fruit, seeds, and even a bit of dark chocolate for a little indulgence. The combination of protein, healthy fats, and carbohydrates will give you the sustained energy you need to tackle any trail.

If you're looking for something a bit more substantial, consider making homemade granola bars. Not only are they easy to make, but they can be packed with nutritious ingredients like oats, nuts, and seeds. You can even customize them with ingredients like dried berries or coconut flakes for added flavor.

For a quick and easy snack, jerky is a great option. You can make your own jerky using lean meats like beef or turkey. Add some seasonings and marinate the meat overnight, then use a dehydrator to remove the moisture. The result is a protein-packed snack that's perfect for on-the-go.

Now, let's satisfy your sweet tooth with some indulgent dehydrated desserts. Just because you're in the wilderness doesn't mean you can't enjoy a sweet treat. Dehydrated desserts are not only delicious but also lightweight and easy to pack.

One option is dehydrated fruit, which can be a refreshing and healthy dessert. You can choose a variety of fruits like apples, bananas, or strawberries, and dehydrate them until they become crispy and flavorful. These make for a sweet and satisfying snack that you can enjoy at any time.

If you're craving something a bit more decadent, try making dehydrated cookies. Simply prepare your favorite cookie dough recipe and spoon small dollops onto a dehydrator tray. Dehydrate them until they become crispy and chewy, and you'll have a tasty dessert that can be enjoyed on the trail.

With these energy-boosting snacks and indulgent dehydrated desserts, you'll be well-equipped for any outdoor adventure. By mastering the art of dehydrating, you can create delicious meals that are lightweight and easy to pack. Meal planning for extended adventures becomes a breeze, as you can preserve food without sacrificing flavor. So pack your backpack, hit the trail, and enjoy the satisfying dining experience that comes with rehydrating meals in the great outdoors.

Chapter 4: The Art of Meal Planning

Strategies for planning meals for extended backpacking trips

Planning meals for extended backpacking trips requires careful consideration of various factors, such as weight, space, and nutritional needs. In this section, we will explore strategies to help you create delicious and nutritious meals that are perfect for your outdoor adventures.

One key technique that can greatly enhance your backpacking meals is the art of dehydrating. Dehydrated food is lightweight, easy to pack, and retains its nutritional value. By dehydrating your own meals, you can customize your menu and ensure that every bite is packed with flavor.

To get started with dehydrating, invest in a good-quality dehydrator or use your oven on a low temperature setting. Choose a variety of fresh ingredients, such as fruits, vegetables, meats, and grains, and cut them into small, uniform pieces. Spread the ingredients in a single layer on dehydrator trays or baking sheets, and let them dry until they are crisp and brittle. Once dehydrated, store the food in airtight containers or vacuum-sealed bags to keep them fresh and ready for your backpacking trips.

Now, let's talk about meal planning. When organizing meals for extended adventures, it's important to consider the length and intensity of your trip. Start by estimating how many meals and snacks you will need for each day, considering the amount of energy you will burn during your activities.

Begin by planning for breakfast, which should provide you with a good amount of energy to kick-start your day. Consider options such as instant oatmeal, granola, or dehydrated breakfast burritos. For lunch and dinner, aim for a balance of carbohydrates, proteins, and healthy fats.

Dehydrated soups, pasta dishes, and stir-fries are great options that can be prepared in advance and rehydrated with boiling water on the trail.

Don't forget about snacks! Having a variety of snacks on hand will help keep your energy levels up throughout the day. Trail mix, energy bars, beef jerky, and dried fruit are all lightweight and easy to carry options.

When meal planning, it's crucial to consider your nutritional needs. Aim for a well-rounded diet that includes a variety of food groups. Include complex carbohydrates for sustained energy, lean proteins for muscle repair and growth, and healthy fats for brain function.

Remember to pack your meals in sealable bags or containers that are lightweight and waterproof. Label each meal with the date and contents to help you stay organized. Lastly, always carry extra food in case of emergency or unexpected delays.

With these strategies and techniques, you can master the art of meal planning for extended backpacking trips. Enjoy delicious, nutritious meals on the trail, and make the most of your outdoor adventures!

Creating a balanced and nutritious meal plan

Now that we understand the importance of a balanced diet for sustained energy, let's dive into the process of creating a balanced and nutritious meal plan for your dehydrated meals. Meal planning plays a crucial role in ensuring that you have all the essential nutrients you need while backpacking or camping.

When planning your meals, it's important to incorporate a variety of essential nutrients to support your energy levels and overall well-being. Here are some tips to help you create a balanced and nutritious meal plan:

1. **Include a source of protein:** Protein is essential for muscle repair and growth. Incorporate protein-rich foods like dehydrated beans, lentils, chicken, or beef into your meal plan.

These will provide a satisfying and filling component to your meals.

2. **Don't forget about carbohydrates:** Carbohydrates are your body's primary source of energy. Include dehydrated grains, such as rice or quinoa, as well as dehydrated fruits and vegetables, which are rich in complex carbohydrates. These will give you the sustained energy you need for your outdoor adventures.

3. **Add healthy fats:** Healthy fats help to provide long-lasting energy and support brain function. Include dehydrated nuts, seeds, and oils in your meal plan to provide a good source of healthy fats. These also add great flavor and crunch to your meals.

4. **Include vitamins and minerals:** It's important to get a variety of vitamins and minerals while on your outdoor adventures. Consider incorporating dehydrated fruits and vegetables, which are packed with essential nutrients, into your meals. You can also bring along dehydrated herbs and spices to add flavor and extra nutrients to your dishes.

5. **Stay hydrated:** Hydration is key when participating in outdoor activities. Remember to stay hydrated by bringing along plenty of water or other hydrating beverages. You can also include dehydrated soup mixes or electrolyte drinks in your meal plan to replenish your fluids.

By following these tips and incorporating a variety of nutrient-rich foods into your dehydrated meal plan, you can ensure that you stay energized and nourished during your extended adventures in the great outdoors.

Tips for efficient meal preparation while on the trail

When it comes to outdoor activities, one of the biggest challenges we face is preparing meals. Luckily, there are ways to streamline the process and save both time and energy. In this subchapter, I will share some tips for efficient meal preparation while on the trail, so you can focus more on enjoying your adventure and less on cooking.

To start, let's talk about the art of dehydrating for backpacking and camping. Dehydrating your meals is a great way to save weight and extend the shelf life of your food. By removing the water content, you can significantly reduce the weight of your ingredients without sacrificing flavor. I'll walk you through the steps of dehydrating different types of foods, from fruits and vegetables to meats and grains. Get ready to create mouthwatering meals that are perfect for the outdoors!

Preserving food without sacrificing flavor is a key skill to learn when it comes to outdoor cooking. I'll show you some effective techniques to ensure your meals stay fresh and tasty for longer periods. From canning to freezing, there are various methods you can use to preserve your ingredients. Say goodbye to spoiled food and hello to delicious meals, even on extended adventures.

Meal planning is essential for any outdoor trip, especially when you're going on extended adventures. I'll guide you through the process of creating a well-balanced menu that meets both your nutritional needs and taste preferences. With proper meal planning, you can save time and avoid the stress of deciding what to cook each day. Plus, I'll share some tips on how to pack and organize your ingredients for easy and convenient cooking.

Weight and space are precious commodities when hiking or backpacking. I'll reveal secrets to save weight and space in your backpack without compromising nutrition. From choosing lightweight cooking equipment to packing compact ingredients, you'll learn how to make the most of your limited resources. Now you can focus on enjoying the outdoors, knowing your meals are both nutritious and easy to carry.

Lastly, let's unlock the secrets to rehydrating meals for a satisfying dining experience. Rehydrating dehydrated meals can sometimes be a tricky process, but with the right techniques, you'll be able to enjoy delicious and nourishing food even when you're far away from a kitchen. I'll share some tips and tricks to ensure your rehydrated meals turn out flavorful and enjoyable.

So get ready to become a master of outdoor meal preparation! With the knowledge and skills you'll gain from this subchapter, you'll be able to create delicious meals that fuel your adventures and leave your taste buds satisfied. Let's dive in!

Chapter 5: Maximizing Nutrition in Dehydrated Meals

Preserving nutrients during the dehydration process

During the dehydration process, it is crucial to preserve the nutritional value of foods. After all, when we go backpacking and camping, we rely on these meals to fuel our bodies and keep us going in the great outdoors. In this subchapter, I'll share some effective techniques to help you retain those important nutrients while dehydrating your meals.

Firstly, it's important to consider the temperature at which you dehydrate your foods. High temperatures can lead to nutrient loss, so it's best to dehydrate at lower temperatures if possible. This may take longer, but it will help to preserve those essential vitamins and minerals.

Another technique to retain nutritional value is to blanch your fruits and vegetables before dehydration. Blanching, which involves briefly boiling or steaming the produce, can help to halt the enzyme activity that can lead to nutrient degradation. After blanching, quickly cool the produce in ice water to preserve its color and texture.

Choosing the right produce for dehydration is also important. Opt for fruits and vegetables that are at their peak ripeness and freshness. These will have higher nutrient content than those that are overripe or past their prime. You can also consider using organic varieties, which tend to have more nutrients due to the absence of pesticides and other harmful chemicals.

In addition to careful temperature control and produce selection, you can also consider adding a small amount of lemon juice to your fruits before dehydrating them. The citric acid in the lemon juice can help to preserve the color and flavor of the fruit, while also providing a boost of vitamin C.

Lastly, remember that dehydration can cause some nutrient loss no matter how careful you are. However, by taking these steps to minimize degradation, you can ensure that your dehydrated meals still pack a nutritional punch when you're out on your adventures.

Incorporating a variety of food groups into dehydrated meals

When it comes to dehydrated meal planning, it's important to strike the right balance between carbohydrates, proteins, and fats. These macronutrients are essential for providing energy, maintaining muscle mass, and supporting overall health during your backpacking or camping adventures.

Carbohydrates are the body's primary source of fuel, so it's crucial to include them in your meals. Opt for complex carbohydrates like whole grains, which release energy slowly and keep you feeling satisfied for longer periods of time. Quinoa, brown rice, and oats are excellent options that can be easily dehydrated and rehydrated.

Proteins are essential for repairing and building muscle tissue, especially after a strenuous hike or physical activity. Incorporating sources of protein into your dehydrated meals is essential. You can dehydrate lean meats like chicken or turkey, or consider plant-based options like beans, lentils, or tofu. These protein-packed ingredients will keep you feeling strong and satisfied throughout your outdoor adventures.

Fats are a concentrated source of energy and play a crucial role in storing and utilizing vitamins and minerals. While it's essential to include healthy fats in your diet, it's important to choose options that are lightweight and suitable for dehydrating. Nuts, seeds, and avocados are excellent choices that provide a good balance of healthy fats and essential nutrients.

In addition to balancing macronutrients, it's also important to incorporate fruits, vegetables, and grains into your dehydrated meals to create a well-rounded diet. These food groups provide important micronutrients like vitamins, minerals, and antioxidants that support overall health and well-being.

Fruits are a great source of vitamins and natural sugars, providing a burst of energy and delicious sweetness. Dehydrated fruits like bananas, apples, and berries can be easily added to your meals or enjoyed as snacks.

Vegetables are packed with essential vitamins, minerals, and fiber. Dehydrated vegetables like carrots, peas, and bell peppers can be rehydrated and added to your main meals for added nutrition and flavor.

Grains like quinoa, rice, and couscous are versatile and can be easily incorporated into dehydrated meals. These complex carbohydrates provide sustained energy and can be cooked and dehydrated in advance for convenient meal planning.

By incorporating a variety of food groups into your dehydrated meals, you'll be able to fuel your body with the necessary nutrients for extended adventures. Plus, these vibrant and flavorful ingredients will enhance the overall taste of your meals, making your dining experience in the wilderness even more enjoyable.

Making informed choices for a well-rounded diet while camping

Now that you've learned the basics of dehydrating foods for your outdoor adventures, it's important to consider dietary restrictions and preferences when selecting your dehydrated meals. After all, just because you're camping doesn't mean you have to sacrifice flavor and nutrition!

If you or someone in your camping group has specific dietary restrictions, such as being vegetarian or gluten-free, it's essential to choose dehydrated foods that cater to those needs. Many companies offer a variety of options that meet different dietary requirements, so be sure to read labels carefully and look for certifications or seals that indicate a product is suitable for your needs.

Additionally, consider your personal preferences when selecting dehydrated meals. Do you have any favorite dishes or flavors that you'd like to enjoy while camping? Look for options that align with your taste preferences to ensure a satisfying dining experience in the great outdoors.

Now that you have a better understanding of how to select dehydrated meals, let's explore some tips for incorporating essential vitamins and minerals into your outdoor meals. Maintaining a well-rounded diet while camping is crucial for overall health and energy levels during your adventures.

One way to ensure you're getting the necessary nutrients is to pack a variety of dehydrated fruits and vegetables. These ingredients not only provide essential vitamins and minerals but also add flavor and texture to your meals. Consider including options like dehydrated peas, berries, kale, and carrots to incorporate a range of nutrients into your camping menu.

Another tip is to pack dehydrated meats or plant-based protein sources, such as lentils or tofu. Protein is essential for repairing and building tissues, especially after long hikes or strenuous activities. Including protein-rich ingredients in your meals will help fuel your adventures and keep you feeling satisfied.

Finally, don't forget about carbohydrates. They are your body's main source of energy, so it's important to include them in your camping meals. Pack dehydrated grains like rice or quinoa, as well as starchy vegetables like potatoes or corn. These options will provide the energy you need to tackle those outdoor activities.

By considering dietary restrictions and preferences and incorporating essential vitamins and minerals into your dehydrated meals, you'll be well on your way to enjoying delicious and nutritious dishes during your outdoor adventures.

Chapter 6: Rehydrating Meals for Optimal Flavor

Methods for rehydrating dehydrated foods

Now that you've learned the basics of dehydrating food for your outdoor adventures, it's time to master the art of rehydrating those meals for a satisfying dining experience. In this subchapter, I'll share with you some effective methods for rehydrating dehydrated foods.

When it comes to rehydration, different types of foods require different approaches. Let's explore some step-by-step instructions for rehydrating various types of foods:

To rehydrate dehydrated fruits, start by placing your desired amount of fruits in a bowl and covering them with water. Let the fruits soak for at least 15 minutes or until they have absorbed enough water to regain their plumpness. Drain any excess water and enjoy!

Rehydrating dehydrated vegetables is similar to rehydrating fruits. Place your vegetables in a bowl and cover them with water. Let them soak for about 30 minutes or until they have softened. Drain the water and your vegetables are now ready to be used in your meals.

Rehydrating dehydrated meat or protein sources, such as beans or tofu, requires a bit more time. Start by adding the desired amount of meat or protein to a bowl and covering it with water. Let it sit for at least 1 hour or until it has rehydrated completely. Drain any excess water and your protein source is ready to be cooked or eaten as is.

When it comes to rehydrating dehydrated grains and pasta, the key is to add hot water instead of cold water. Place your desired amount of grains or pasta in a bowl and cover them with boiling water. Let them sit for about 10-15 minutes or until they have softened. Drain any excess water and your grains or pasta are now ready to be seasoned and enjoyed.

To rehydrate dehydrated soups and stews, it's best to follow the instructions provided on the packaging. Typically, you'll need to bring water to a boil and then add the contents of the package. Let it simmer for the recommended time and stir occasionally. Once the ingredients have rehydrated and the flavors have melded together, your delicious soup or stew is ready to be enjoyed.

Now that you know how to rehydrate different types of foods, let's discuss some best practices to ensure even rehydration and enjoyable texture.

It's important to use the appropriate amount of water when rehydrating your meals. Adding too much water can result in a mushy texture, while adding too little water can leave your food dry and undercooked. Follow the recommended water-to-food ratio provided on the packaging or adjust it to your personal preference.

While rehydrating your meals, it's a good idea to give them a stir every now and then. This helps distribute the water evenly and ensures that all the ingredients rehydrate properly.

Patience is key when it comes to rehydrating your meals. Make sure to give your food enough time to fully rehydrate and absorb the water. This may require different amounts of time depending on the type of food, so always refer to the instructions or use your judgment.

By following these methods and best practices, you'll be able to rehydrate your dehydrated meals to perfection. Enjoy your flavorful and nutritious outdoor dining experiences!

Enhancing flavor and texture during the rehydration process

Now that you've learned the basics of dehydrating food, it's time to take your culinary skills to the next level. In this section, I'll share some tips and techniques for enhancing the flavor and texture of your rehydrated meals. By following these strategies, you'll be able to create mouthwatering dishes that are perfect for your outdoor adventures.

When it comes to rehydrating meals, there are several ways to enhance the flavor and make them more enjoyable to eat. One of the simplest ways to do this is by adding seasonings and spices. These can add depth and complexity to your meals, transforming them from bland to delicious.

Experiment with different combinations of herbs, spices, and seasonings to find the flavors that you enjoy the most. Some popular options include garlic powder, onion powder, dried herbs like oregano or thyme, and spice blends like curry powder or chili powder.

To get the most flavor out of your seasonings, consider rehydrating them along with your meals. This allows the flavors to meld together and infuse into the food. Simply add the desired spices and seasonings to your water or liquid before you rehydrate your meal. This way, the flavors will be absorbed during the rehydration process, resulting in a more flavorful dish.

In addition to enhancing the flavor of your rehydrated meals, it's also important to pay attention to the texture and consistency. Nobody wants to eat something that's mushy or overly dry. So, let's explore some techniques to achieve the desired texture of your meals.

One technique is to adjust the amount of water you use for rehydration. If you prefer a softer texture, use more water or liquid. On the other hand, if you like your food to have a firmer texture, use less water. By experimenting with the water-to-food ratio, you can achieve the ideal consistency for each meal.

Another technique is to let your meals rehydrate for the proper amount of time. Follow the instructions on the packaging or recipe to determine the recommended rehydration time. Under-hydrating or over-hydrating can result in a less-than-ideal texture. So, be patient and let your meals soak for the specified duration.

Lastly, consider adding ingredients that can help improve the texture of your meals. For example, adding a small amount of oil or butter can make your food creamier and more enjoyable to eat. Similarly, adding crunchy toppings like toasted nuts or breadcrumbs can add a satisfying texture contrast.

The importance of proper hydration for rehydrated meals

As we delve deeper into the world of rehydrated meals for outdoor adventures, one key component that cannot be overlooked is proper hydration. Understanding the role of hydration is not only essential for our overall well-being but also plays a significant role in maximizing the taste and benefits of rehydrated meals.

When we engage in outdoor activities, our bodies lose water through sweat and exertion. Dehydration can occur quickly, leading to decreased performance, fatigue, and even more serious health issues. That's why it's crucial to prioritize adequate water intake throughout your adventure.

So, why is hydration so important when it comes to rehydrated meals? Well, let me share with you a few reasons.

First and foremost, maintaining proper hydration ensures that our bodies function optimally. Water is essential for digestion, absorption of nutrients, and the elimination of waste products. When we are well-hydrated, our bodies can efficiently process and utilize the nutrients from our meals, enhancing their overall flavor and benefits.

Furthermore, dehydration can affect our taste buds and perception of flavor. Have you ever noticed that food doesn't taste as good when you're dehydrated? That's because dehydration can dull our sense of taste and make it more challenging to fully appreciate the flavors of our rehydrated meals.

Lastly, staying hydrated improves the rehydration process itself. When we add water to our dehydrated meals, having a well-hydrated body aids in the absorption and reconstitution of the ingredients. This ensures that the flavors are evenly distributed and the texture is just right, resulting in a satisfying dining experience.

Now that we understand the importance of proper hydration for rehydrated meals, let's dive into some practical tips to ensure we're getting enough water during our outdoor activities.

Firstly, it's essential to have easy access to water throughout your adventure. Whether you're hiking, backpacking, or camping, always carry an adequate supply of water or have a reliable method of purifying water from natural sources.

Secondly, make it a habit to drink water regularly, even if you don't feel thirsty. Thirst is not always an accurate indicator of our hydration status, so sipping water throughout the day is crucial.

Additionally, consider adding flavor to your water to make it more enticing. Infusing water with fruits, herbs, or electrolyte mixes can not only enhance the taste but also provide additional benefits and encourage you to drink more.

Lastly, monitor your urine color as a quick and simple way to assess your hydration level. Aim for a pale yellow color, indicating that you're adequately hydrated. If your urine is dark yellow or amber, increase your water intake immediately.

By following these tips and prioritizing hydration during your outdoor adventures, you'll not only maximize the taste and benefits of your rehydrated meals but also ensure that you're performing at your best and enjoying every moment of your journey.

Chapter 7: Food Safety Considerations

Understanding food safety principles for dehydrating

When it comes to dehydrating food for your outdoor adventures, practicing good hygiene and sanitation is absolutely crucial. It's not just about preserving the flavor and nutritional value of the food, but also ensuring that you and your fellow adventurers stay healthy and safe throughout your journey.

Proper sanitation starts from the moment you start handling the ingredients. Wash your hands thoroughly with soap and water before touching any food items. This simple step helps prevent the spread of harmful bacteria and contaminants. Additionally, make sure all the utensils and equipment you use for dehydrating are clean and sanitized before use.

Cleanliness should also extend to the workspace where you prepare and dehydrate your meals. Keep countertops and cutting boards clean, and sanitize them regularly. It's a good practice to designate specific areas for handling raw and cooked foods to avoid cross-contamination.

When dehydrating meals for the outdoors, preventing cross-contamination is crucial to avoid the risk of foodborne illnesses. Cross-contamination occurs when bacteria or other pathogens from one food item are transferred to another.

To prevent cross-contamination, always keep raw and cooked foods separate. Use separate cutting boards and utensils for raw meats and vegetables. If possible, use color-coded cutting boards to easily differentiate between different food groups. Also, make sure to wash these items thoroughly with hot, soapy water after each use.

Another way to prevent cross-contamination is by properly storing your dehydrated meals. Use airtight containers or vacuum-sealed bags to keep your meals fresh and free from any potential contaminants. Label the containers with the date and contents to ensure you know when they were prepared and what they contain.

Understanding food safety principles for dehydrating

When it comes to dehydrating food, it's important to understand food safety principles to ensure that your meals are safe to consume. Here are a few key principles to keep in mind:

- Temperature control: Dehydrating food at the proper temperature is essential to kill harmful bacteria and prevent the growth of microorganisms. Make sure your dehydrator is set to the recommended temperature for each type of food.
- Proper storage: Once your meals are dehydrated, it's important to store them properly to maintain their quality and safety. Store them in cool, dry, and dark places to prevent the growth of bacteria and mold.
- Hydration process: When you're ready to enjoy your dehydrated meals, it's important to rehydrate them properly. Follow the instructions provided for each meal, and make sure to use clean water. If you're backpacking or camping in an area with questionable water quality, it's best to bring your own filtered or purified water.

Preventing foodborne illness while preparing and consuming dehydrated meals

When it comes to preparing and consuming dehydrated meals, it's important to take steps to prevent foodborne illnesses. In this section, I'll share some valuable tips on how you can ensure the safety of your dehydrated food while enjoying the convenience and deliciousness it offers.

Safe Storage and Handling Techniques:

Proper storage and handling are essential to avoid bacterial growth in dehydrated foods. By following these techniques, you can keep your meals safe and hygienic:

- Store dehydrated foods in airtight containers or vacuum-sealed bags to prevent moisture and air exposure, which can lead to bacterial growth.
- Keep dehydrated foods in a cool, dry place away from direct sunlight. Excessive heat and moisture can cause spoilage and reduce the shelf life of your meals.
- Label your containers with the date of dehydration to ensure you consume them within a reasonable timeframe.
- Regularly inspect your dehydrated foods for signs of spoilage, such as mold, off odors, or discoloration. Throw away any food that appears questionable.
- Practice good hygiene when handling dehydrated foods. Wash your hands before and after touching them to prevent cross-contamination.

Tips for Proper Rehydration:
Rehydrating dehydrated meals is a crucial step to ensure their safety and palatability. Here are some tips to follow for a satisfying and risk-free dining experience:

- Follow the instructions provided with your dehydrated meals for the recommended rehydration method and ratios of water to food.
- Boil the water used for rehydration to kill any potential pathogens and ensure the safety of your meal.
- Allow enough time for thorough rehydration. Rushing the process may result in an unevenly rehydrated meal or the persistence of harmful bacteria.
- Stir or shake the mixture periodically during the rehydration

process to promote even absorption of water and prevent clumping.

- Test the readiness of your rehydrated meal by sampling a small portion. Make sure it is fully rehydrated and has a pleasant texture before consuming the entire meal.

By implementing these safe storage and rehydration techniques, you can enjoy delicious and nutritious dehydrated meals without compromising your health. In the next section, we'll explore the art of meal planning specifically for extended outdoor adventures, so stay tuned!

Storage and shelf-life considerations for dehydrated foods

Now that you've learned about the basics of dehydrating meals for your outdoor adventures, it's time to dive deeper into the storage and shelf-life considerations for dehydrated foods. This is an important aspect to ensure that your meals maintain their quality and safety throughout your trip.

When it comes to storing dehydrated meals, there are a few best practices that you should keep in mind. First and foremost, it's crucial to store your dehydrated food in a cool and dry place. Exposure to heat and moisture can lead to spoilage and the growth of bacteria, which can be harmful if consumed.

One effective technique for preserving dehydrated food is to use airtight containers or vacuum-sealed bags. These containers help to keep out any moisture and oxygen, which can cause the food to spoil faster. It's also a good idea to label each container with the date of dehydration, so that you can keep track of its shelf life.

Another important consideration is to store your dehydrated meals away from direct sunlight. Sunlight can cause the food to degrade and lose its nutritional value. Therefore, it's best to choose a dark storage area or use opaque containers that block out light.

Understanding the shelf life of dehydrated foods is key to ensuring that you consume them at their best quality. Most dehydrated meals have a shelf life of several months to a year, depending on the type of food and the storage conditions. It's important to check the packaging or consult the manufacturer's guidelines for specific shelf life information.

However, it's important to note that even though dehydrated foods can have a long shelf life, they can still eventually spoil. It's crucial to regularly inspect your stored dehydrated meals for any signs of spoilage, such as mold, off odors, or a change in color or texture. If you notice any of these signs, it's best to discard the food to avoid any potential health risks.

By following these best practices for storing and preserving dehydrated meals, you can ensure that your meals remain safe and delicious throughout your outdoor adventures. With proper storage techniques and a good understanding of shelf life, you can enjoy the convenience and flavors of dehydrated meals without compromising quality.

Chapter 8: Preserving Freshness and Flavor

Techniques for maintaining the quality of dehydrated foods over time

As a fellow outdoor enthusiast, I know just how important it is to pack and store your dehydrated foods properly to ensure they stay fresh and delicious on your adventures. In this section, I'll share with you my top tips for preventing oxidation and moisture absorption in your dehydrated meals.

- Choose the right packaging: Opt for airtight containers such as resealable bags or vacuum-sealed pouches to keep air out and prevent oxidation. Mason jars can also work well if you plan to consume the food within a shorter timeframe.
- Use oxygen absorbers: These small packets contain iron powder that absorbs oxygen, helping to extend the shelf life of your dehydrated foods. Place one or two absorbers in each packaging before sealing to keep your meals fresh.
- Avoid moisture: Moisture is the enemy when it comes to preserving dehydrated foods. Make sure your food is completely dry before packaging it, as even a small amount of moisture can lead to mold or spoilage. If necessary, use a food dehydrator or low-temperature oven to remove any remaining moisture.
- Keep it cool and dark: Store your dehydrated meals in a cool, dark place to protect them from heat and light. Excessive exposure to light and heat can degrade the quality and taste of the food.
- Label and rotate: Properly label each package with the contents and date of dehydration to ensure you consume your oldest

meals first. This will help you avoid any potential wastage.

Now that you know how to properly package and store your dehydrated foods, let's dive into some tips for extending their freshness and flavor. These techniques will make sure your meals taste as amazing as they did the day you made them.

- Choose high-quality ingredients: The flavor and quality of your dehydrated meals largely depend on the ingredients you use. Be selective and opt for fresh, seasonal produce and lean meats to create mouthwatering dishes.
- Add spices and herbs: Don't be afraid to get creative with your spices and herbs. They not only enhance the flavor but also provide additional health benefits. Experiment with different combinations to find your favorite flavors.
- Pre-treat ingredients: Some ingredients, such as fruits prone to browning, benefit from pre-treatment before dehydrating. You can dip them in lemon juice or blanch them briefly to maintain their color and texture.
- Store meals in portion sizes: Instead of packaging your dehydrated meals as one big batch, divide them into individual portion sizes. This way, you can easily grab a meal for one person without having to rehydrate the entire batch.
- Consider meal planning: Planning your meals in advance can save you time and effort on your adventures. Create a meal plan to ensure you have a variety of delicious options to choose from, and pack your dehydrated meals accordingly.
- Rehydrate with care: The rehydration process is crucial to transforming your dehydrated meals into satisfying dishes. Follow the recommended instructions for adding water and allow sufficient time for the ingredients to rehydrate fully.

Tips for preserving flavor and texture in dehydrated

meals

Now that you've mastered the art of dehydrating your meals for backpacking and camping, it's time to take your culinary skills to the next level. In this subchapter, I'll share some valuable tips for preserving flavor and texture in your dehydrated meals, ensuring that every bite is a mouthwatering delight.

When it comes to dehydrating meals, the choice of ingredients plays a crucial role in preserving the natural flavors of the foods. Opt for fresh, high-quality produce and lean proteins. This will ensure that your meals are bursting with taste. Don't be afraid to get creative with your ingredients. Add herbs, spices, and flavorful sauces to enhance the overall flavor profile of your meals.

Another important factor in preserving flavor is the preparation method. Avoid overcooking your ingredients before dehydrating them. While it's essential to fully cook meats and vegetables for safety reasons, make sure not to overcook them, as this can result in a loss of flavor and texture. Aim to cook your ingredients until they are just tender, and then dehydrate them promptly.

Now, let's talk about some common pitfalls that can affect the taste and texture of dehydrated meals. First and foremost, be mindful of the moisture content in your meals. Excess moisture can lead to spoilage and a reduction in flavor. Make sure to dehydrate your meals thoroughly, following the recommended time and temperature guidelines for each ingredient.

Furthermore, be careful not to overcrowd the dehydrator trays. Proper air circulation is essential for even drying. If the airflow is restricted, you may end up with unevenly dehydrated ingredients, resulting in variations in taste and texture. It's better to dehydrate in multiple batches if needed, to ensure optimal results.

Lastly, storing your dehydrated meals correctly will help maintain their flavor and texture over time. Store them in airtight containers or vacuum-sealed bags in a cool, dry place. Avoid exposing them to sunlight or moisture, as this can degrade the quality of the food.

By following these tips and techniques, you'll be able to create dehydrated meals that are not only perfect for the outdoors but also bursting with flavor. So, let's get started and elevate your camping and backpacking meals to a whole new level of deliciousness!

How to avoid common pitfalls that can affect the quality of dehydrated foods

In the exciting world of backpacking and camping, mastering the art of dehydrating food opens up a world of mouthwatering meals that are perfect for the great outdoors. As you embark on your culinary journey, it's important to be aware of common pitfalls that can affect the quality of your dehydrated foods. By avoiding these pitfalls, you can preserve the flavor and nutrition of your meals, ensuring a satisfying dining experience every time.

One common issue that can arise during the dehydration process is uneven drying. To prevent this, make sure to cut your food into uniform sizes. This will ensure that all pieces dehydrate at the same rate, resulting in consistent texture and doneness. Additionally, be mindful of the thickness of your slices. Thicker slices take longer to dehydrate, so adjust your drying time accordingly.

Another issue to watch out for is over-drying. While you want your food to be thoroughly dehydrated to prevent spoilage, it's important not to go too far. Over-dried food can become brittle and lose its flavor. To avoid this, keep a close eye on your dehydrator or oven temperature and drying time. Regularly check the progress of your food and remove it from the dehydrator or oven as soon as it is adequately dried.

In addition to these tips, it's crucial to properly store your dehydrated food. Moisture is the enemy when it comes to food preservation, so make sure your dehydrated meals are stored in airtight containers or vacuum-sealed bags. This will prevent moisture from re-entering the food and causing spoilage. Store your containers in a cool, dark place to further prolong the shelf life of your dehydrated meals.

Now that you're equipped with the knowledge to avoid common pitfalls, it's time to take your dehydrated meals into challenging outdoor conditions. When backpacking or camping, it's important to maintain the quality of your dehydrated food. One way to do this is by practicing effective meal planning for extended adventures. Plan your meals ahead of time, taking into consideration the duration of your trip and the nutritional needs of your body. This will help you avoid running out of food or relying on unhealthy snacks during your outdoor adventures.

Another tip for maintaining the quality of your dehydrated meals in challenging outdoor conditions is to save weight and space in your backpack without compromising nutrition. Dehydrated foods are lightweight and compact, making them ideal for backpacking. However, it's important to choose nutrient-dense ingredients that will fuel your body during strenuous outdoor activities. Opt for foods high in protein, healthy fats, and complex carbohydrates to keep your energy levels up.

Lastly, when it comes time to enjoy your dehydrated meals, unlocking the secrets to rehydrating is key. Follow the instructions provided with your specific meals, as the rehydration method may vary depending on the ingredients used. Generally, adding hot water and allowing the meal to sit for a specified amount of time will rehydrate the food to its original state. Stirring occasionally can help distribute the water evenly.

By following these tips and techniques, you'll be well on your way to becoming a master of dehydrated meals for backpacking and camping. Enjoy the convenience and deliciousness of homemade dehydrated food while exploring the great outdoors!

Chapter 9: Sustainable and Eco-friendly Practices

Minimizing food waste through dehydrating

When it comes to reducing food waste, dehydrating surplus produce and leftovers is a fantastic strategy. Not only does it help to extend the shelf life of your food, but it also allows you to create delicious meals even when you're out backpacking or camping. In this subchapter, we'll explore some tips and techniques to minimize food waste through dehydrating.

The art of dehydrating is an essential skill to learn if you want to create mouthwatering meals that are perfect for the outdoors. By removing the moisture from your food, you not only make it last longer but also reduce its weight, making it easier to carry on extended adventures.

Preserving your food through dehydration doesn't mean sacrificing flavor. In fact, it's quite the opposite. Dehydrating can intensify the natural flavors of your food, resulting in incredibly tasty meals that will satisfy your cravings.

Meal planning is another crucial aspect to master when it comes to minimizing food waste. By carefully planning your meals for your backpacking or camping trips, you can ensure that you utilize all of your dehydrated ingredients effectively, leaving nothing to waste.

One of the great advantages of dehydrating your food is that it saves a lot of space in your backpack. Since dehydrated food weighs significantly less than fresh produce, you can carry a larger quantity without adding extra weight to your load. This leaves more room for other essential items and ensures that you have enough sustenance for your entire adventure.

Now, let's unlock the secrets to rehydrating meals for a satisfying dining experience. Rehydrating dehydrated food requires a bit of finesse, but with the right techniques, you can enjoy hearty, flavorful meals that will leave you feeling nourished and satisfied. We'll explore different methods and tips to ensure that your rehydrated meals turn out delicious every time.

So get ready to embark on a journey of dehydrating, meal planning, and rehydration. By incorporating these strategies into your outdoor adventures, you'll not only save food from going to waste but also create incredible meals that will fuel you for your exciting endeavors.

Choosing sustainably sourced ingredients for dehydrated meals

Choosing sustainably sourced ingredients for dehydrated meals:

Hey there! Now that you've learned the basics of dehydrating for backpacking and camping, it's time to take your skills to the next level by choosing sustainably sourced ingredients for your dehydrated meals. Not only will this help protect the environment, but it will also ensure that you're supporting ethical practices in the food industry.

1. Look for organic options:

When selecting ingredients for your dehydrated meals, consider opting for organic options whenever possible. Organic farming practices prioritize environmental sustainability by avoiding the use of synthetic pesticides and fertilizers. By choosing organic, you're not only supporting the health of the planet but also ensuring that your meals are free from harmful chemicals.

2. Choose locally sourced ingredients:

Another great way to support sustainable practices is by choosing locally sourced ingredients. Locally sourced ingredients have a smaller carbon footprint since they don't need to travel long distances to reach your plate. Additionally, supporting local farmers and producers helps to strengthen your community's food system. So keep an eye out for farmers' markets and local food co-ops where you can find fresh, locally sourced ingredients for your dehydrated meals.

3. Consider the seasonality of ingredients:

Seasonality plays a significant role in sustainable eating. By choosing ingredients that are in season, you're reducing the energy and resources needed to grow and transport them. Out-of-season produce often requires long-distance travel or energy-intensive greenhouses to cultivate, both of which have negative environmental impacts. So, before you start dehydrating, do some research on which ingredients are currently in season and incorporate them into your meals.

4. Support sustainable fishing and farming practices:

If you're including seafood or animal products in your dehydrated meals, it's essential to choose sustainably sourced options. Look for certifications such as the Marine Stewardship Council (MSC) for seafood or the Certified Humane label for animal products. These certifications ensure that the products were caught or raised using sustainable practices that minimize harm to the environment and prioritize animal welfare.

Remember, every small choice you make can have a big impact on the environment and the food industry. So as you embark on your dehydrating adventures, keep these considerations in mind and choose ingredients that align with your values of sustainability and ethical sourcing.

Reducing environmental impact while enjoying outdoor dining

In the previous chapter, we discussed the importance of minimizing waste and preserving natural habitats while enjoying the great outdoors. Now, let's delve into the world of dehydrated meals and explore how we can reduce our environmental impact while still enjoying delicious meals during our outdoor adventures.

When it comes to backpacking and camping, one of the biggest challenges is finding food that is lightweight and easy to carry, without compromising on taste and nutrition. That's where dehydrated meals come in handy.

Dehydrating food is a technique that removes the moisture from ingredients, making them lightweight and compact. This preservation method not only extends the shelf life of food but also retains much of its flavor and nutrients. So, when you're out in the wilderness, you can still enjoy mouthwatering meals that are perfect for the outdoors.

Now, let's dive into some effective techniques to preserve food without sacrificing flavor. One popular method is to dehydrate fruits and vegetables. By removing the water content, you can significantly reduce the weight and bulk of these ingredients without losing out on their natural goodness. Plus, they make for great snacks and add-ons to your meals.

Meal planning is another crucial aspect of reducing our environmental impact while enjoying outdoor dining. By carefully planning your meals in advance, you can ensure that you only carry the necessary ingredients and minimize food waste. Consider creating a menu for your entire trip and pre-measuring ingredients to save time and effort on the trail.

Now, let's talk about rehydrating meals for a satisfying dining experience. This process involves adding water to your dehydrated meals to restore their original texture and flavor. A common mistake is to use too much water, which leads to soggy and watery meals. To avoid this, it's important to follow the instructions provided with your dehydrated meals and experiment with different water-to-meal ratios to find the perfect balance.

As you venture into the world of dehydrated meals, you'll discover that there are various eco-friendly packaging and disposal options available. Look for brands that use minimal packaging and offer compostable options. Additionally, consider repackaging your dehydrated meals into reusable containers to further reduce waste.

By learning the art of dehydrating food, you can save weight and space in your backpack without compromising on nutrition and flavor.

So, let's embark on this culinary adventure and unlock the secrets of creating satisfying meals that are perfect for your outdoor escapades.

Chapter 10: Smarter Packing for Backpacking and Camping

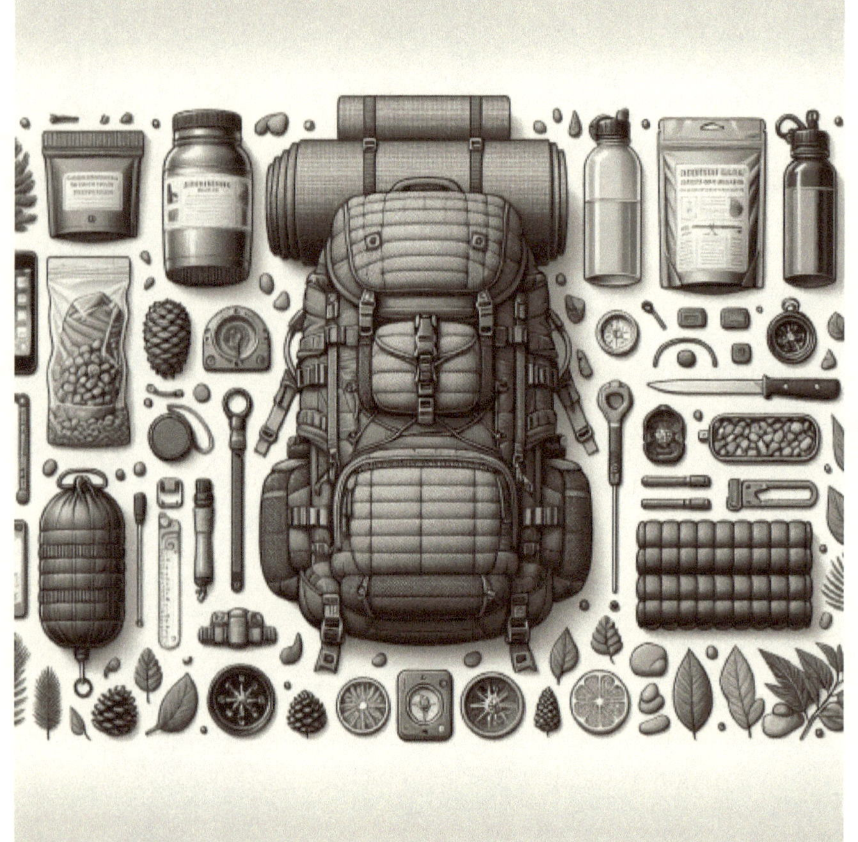

Maximizing space and weight in your backpack with dehydrated meals

I'm excited to share with you some valuable strategies for maximizing space and weight in your backpack with dehydrated meals. When you're out in the wilderness, every ounce counts, and having lightweight and compact meals can make a significant difference in your overall backpack weight.

The first thing to consider is the benefits of lightweight and compact dehydrated meals for backpackers like yourself. Not only do they save on weight, but they also offer great convenience. Dehydrated meals are easy to prepare, often just requiring hot water to rehydrate. They also have a long shelf life, making them a reliable option for extended adventures.

Now, let's delve into some strategies for efficient packing and optimizing storage space.

One effective technique is to carefully plan your meals and pack only what you need for the duration of your trip. This eliminates unnecessary weight and ensures that you have enough food to sustain yourself. Consider the number of meals you'll be having each day and pack accordingly.

Another way to save space is by using lightweight and collapsible containers for your dehydrated meals. Look for durable, food-grade silicone containers that can be easily compressed when empty. This allows you to flatten them and stack them neatly in your backpack.

When it comes to rehydrating your meals, opt for single-serving pouches or use resealable bags. These options not only save space but also allow for easy portion control. Simply pour the required amount of hot water into the pouch or bag and mix well. You'll have a delicious, rehydrated meal ready in no time.

It's also worth mentioning the importance of proper packaging. Make sure to transfer your dehydrated meals into waterproof and airtight bags to protect them from moisture and insects. This will help maintain their quality and prevent any spoilage.

Lastly, take advantage of any empty spaces in your backpack. Use smaller items like utensils, spices, or condiments to fill gaps and prevent your dehydrated meals from shifting during your hike. This will help maximize the space without adding much weight.

I hope these strategies help you save weight and space in your backpack without compromising on nutrition. By using lightweight and compact dehydrated meals and implementing these packing techniques, you'll be able to enjoy mouthwatering meals while embracing the freedom of the great outdoors.

Efficient packing strategies for multi-day hiking trips

is crucial for a successful outdoor adventure. As a seasoned hiker and backpacker, I have discovered some tips and tricks to help you minimize bulk and maximize efficiency in your backpack. Let's dive into some efficient packing strategies for multi-day hiking trips.

Firstly, it is important to consider the weight and space of your backpack. Every once of weight makes a difference when you are trekking for multiple days. One effective way to save weight and space is by dehydrating your meals. Dehydrated meals are lightweight, compact, and easy to rehydrate when you're ready to eat. By dehydrating your own meals, you have control over the ingredients and can create mouthwatering meals that are perfect for the outdoors.

To preserve food without sacrificing flavor, it is important to use effective dehydration techniques. Invest in a good food dehydrator or use the oven on a low temperature to remove moisture from fruits, vegetables, and cooked meals. This process helps to extend the shelf life of the food while maintaining its nutritional value and taste.

Meal planning is another crucial aspect of organizing your supplies for a multi-day hike. Plan your meals in advance, considering the number of days you will be hiking and the nutritional requirements of your body. Pack individual meal portions in ziplock bags or vacuum-sealed bags to keep them fresh and organized. Label each bag with the meal name and the date to ensure you consume them in the right order.

When it comes to saving space in your backpack, try packing items in a systematic manner. Place heavier items closer to your back to distribute the weight evenly. Use compression sacks or packing cubes to separate and compress your gear. This will help you maximize the available space and make it easier to find items when you need them.

Lastly, rehydrating meals properly is essential for a satisfying dining experience on the trail. Follow the instructions provided with your dehydrated meals or experiment with different methods to find what works best for you. Some hikers prefer hot water rehydration, while others opt for cold soaking. Find the method that suits your taste preferences and allows you to enjoy a delicious meal after a long day of hiking.

By implementing these efficient packing strategies, you can save weight and space in your backpack without compromising nutrition. Organizing dehydrated meals and other supplies for easy access will make your multi-day hiking trips more enjoyable and hassle-free. So get ready to embark on your next adventure with a well-organized and efficiently packed backpack! Happy hiking!

Selecting the right packaging for dehydrated foods

Choosing the right packaging for your dehydrated meals plays a crucial role in ensuring that your food stays fresh, lightweight, and durable during your backpacking and camping adventures. In this section, we will explore some key considerations for selecting the perfect packaging options for your dehydrated foods.

One important factor to consider is the weight of the packaging itself. When you're carrying all your gear on your back, every ounce matters. Look for lightweight packaging materials, such as resealable plastic bags or pouches made from durable yet lightweight materials. These options will help you save weight in your backpack without compromising on the durability of the packaging.

Another crucial consideration is the durability of the packaging. As you'll be spending time outdoors, your food packaging needs to be able to withstand rough handling, extreme weather conditions, and potential impacts. Opt for packaging options that are tear-resistant and have strong seals to prevent any leakage or spoilage of your dehydrated meals.

Besides being lightweight and durable, your packaging should also be resealable and waterproof. This is especially important to protect your food from moisture, which can lead to spoilage and the growth of bacteria. Look for packaging options that have airtight seals and are designed to keep out water. This will ensure that your dehydrated meals stay fresh and safe to consume throughout your outdoor adventures.

An additional consideration for your packaging is its size and shape. When you're packing for extended adventures, space becomes a precious commodity. Look for packaging options that can be conveniently stacked or rolled up to maximize your backpack's space. Consider using square or rectangular packaging rather than round containers, as they can fit more efficiently into your backpack.

Lastly, it's worth mentioning the importance of sustainability in your packaging choices. Opt for packaging materials that are eco-friendly and recyclable whenever possible. This will help minimize your environmental impact and contribute to the preservation of the beautiful outdoors that you enjoy exploring.

By choosing lightweight and durable packaging options that are resealable and waterproof, you can ensure that your dehydrated meals stay fresh and safe to consume during your outdoor adventures. These considerations, along with the size, shape, and sustainability of your packaging, will help you save weight and space in your backpack without compromising on the quality and nutrition of your meals.

Chapter 11: Flavor Enhancements and Seasonings

Packing lightweight and versatile seasonings for added flavor

Hey there, fellow outdoor adventurers!

Now that you've learned how to dehydrate meals for backpacking and camping, and discovered the techniques to preserve food without sacrificing flavor, it's time to take your outdoor dining experience to the next level. In this section, we're going to talk about packing lightweight and versatile seasonings to add that extra burst of flavor to your dehydrated meals.

When you're out in the wilderness, every ounce matters. That's why it's important to choose seasonings that are both light in weight and packed with flavor. Here are a few essential spices and seasonings that can elevate the taste of your dehydrated meals:

- Cumin: This aromatic spice adds a warm and earthy flavor to your dishes. It pairs well with many different ingredients and can give your meals a delightful twist.
- Paprika: Whether you prefer sweet, smoked, or hot, paprika is a versatile seasoning that adds a vibrant red color and a mild, smoky flavor to your dishes.
- Garlic powder: A little bit of garlic powder goes a long way in enhancing the taste of your meals. It adds a savory and slightly tangy flavor that complements a variety of ingredients.
- Dried herbs: Herbs like basil, oregano, and thyme can add freshness and complexity to your meals. Just a sprinkle of these dried herbs can make a world of difference.
- Salt and pepper: These classic seasonings are a must-have in any kitchen, and the same goes for the outdoors. They can enhance

the flavors of your meals and bring out the natural taste of the other ingredients.

- Hot sauce or chili flakes: If you like a bit of heat in your meals, don't forget to pack some hot sauce or chili flakes. They can add a spicy kick to your dishes and take them to a whole new level.

Now that you know the essential spices and seasonings to pack, let's talk about creating flavor combinations that will make your outdoor dining experience truly enjoyable. Here are some tips to keep in mind:

- Consider the main ingredient: Think about the dominant flavor of your dehydrated meal and choose seasonings that will enhance it. For example, if you're making a pasta dish, you might want to add some Italian herbs like basil and oregano.
- Experiment with different cuisines: Don't be afraid to try out seasonings from different cuisines to add variety to your meals. You can explore flavors from Mexican, Asian, or Mediterranean cuisine to spice things up.
- Balance the flavors: Aim for a well-balanced meal by combining different flavors like sweet, salty, savory, and spicy. This will make your meals more satisfying and enjoyable.
- Bring small containers: Rather than carrying large bottles of seasonings, transfer small amounts of each spice or seasoning into lightweight and airtight containers. This will help you save space and keep your pack weight down.
- Label your containers: It's a good idea to label your seasoning containers so that you can easily identify them and avoid any mix-ups. You don't want to accidentally add chili flakes instead of paprika to your meal!

There you have it, some essential spices and seasonings to elevate the taste of your dehydrated meals, along with tips for creating flavor combinations. Remember, the key is to pack light, choose versatile seasonings, and get creative with your flavors. Happy cooking and happy trails!

Enhancing dehydrated meals with herbs and spices

As we dive deeper into the world of dehydrated meals, it's important to understand how we can enhance their flavors using herbs and spices. In this subchapter, we will explore creative ways to use these natural ingredients to add variety and depth to your outdoor meals. Get ready to take your taste buds on an adventure!

Incorporating ethnic flavors into outdoor dining

Welcome back! In this section, we'll dive into the exciting world of incorporating ethnic flavors into outdoor dining. Whether you're a backpacker, a camper, or simply enjoy dining al fresco, there's something truly special about savoring international flavors while surrounded by nature. With a bit of creativity and planning, you can recreate your favorite global cuisines in dehydrated meals that are perfect for your outdoor adventures.

When it comes to outdoor dining, it's all about saving weight and space in your backpack without compromising on nutrition or flavor. Dehydrating your meals is a fantastic way to achieve this, as it allows you to preserve food while retaining its distinctive flavors. Plus, with effective techniques, you can rehydrate your meals for a satisfying dining experience that truly transports you to culinary destinations around the world.

So, how can you incorporate those mouthwatering ethnic flavors into your outdoor meals? Here are some tips to get you started:

- Research seasoning profiles: Before embarking on your outdoor adventure, take the time to explore the distinct seasoning profiles of different global cuisines. Each cuisine has its own unique blend of herbs, spices, and condiments that give their dishes their signature taste. Understanding these flavor profiles will help you recreate them in your dehydrated meals.

- Experiment with spices and herbs: Once you've familiarized yourself with various flavor profiles, don't be afraid to get creative with your spice and herb choices. Consider using popular spices like cumin, turmeric, paprika, or garam masala to infuse your meals with Indian flavors. Or, try herbs such as basil, oregano, and thyme to capture the essence of Mediterranean cuisine.

- Incorporate specialty ingredients: To truly elevate your outdoor dining experience, consider incorporating specialty ingredients that are commonly used in specific cuisines. For example, soy sauce, sesame oil, and ginger can help you achieve the umami-packed flavors of Asian cuisine. Dried chiles, lime, and cilantro can bring the vibrant tastes of Mexican dishes to your plate.

- Get creative with marinades: If you have a bit more time before your trip, try marinating your meat or vegetables with ethnic-inspired marinades. This will infuse them with flavor and make your outdoor meals even more delicious. Think of classics like teriyaki for an Asian twist or a tangy Greek marinade for a taste of the Mediterranean.

- Don't forget about sauces: Sauces can be a game-changer when it comes to adding ethnic flavors to your dehydrated meals. Consider making small batches of sauces like pesto, curry, or salsa verde to drizzle over your rehydrated dishes. They will bring that extra burst of flavor and authenticity.

As you embark on your outdoor culinary journey, remember that the key is to experiment, have fun, and get inspired by the diverse cuisines from around the world. With a little bit of planning and a dash of creativity, you can create dehydrated meals that will transport you to far-off places with every delicious bite. Happy cooking and happy trails!

Chapter 12: Dehydrating Fruits and Vegetables

Techniques for dehydrating a variety of fruits

In this subchapter, we will explore different techniques for dehydrating a variety of fruits. Whether you're preparing for a backpacking or camping trip, or simply want to learn the art of dehydrating, these methods will help you create mouthwatering meals that are perfect for the outdoors.

Let's start with some popular fruits like apples, bananas, and berries. Each of these fruits requires a slightly different approach to achieve the best dehydrated result.

For apples, start by slicing them into thin rounds or wedges. You can choose to peel them or leave the skin on for added texture. Lay the slices on the dehydrator trays, making sure they don't overlap. Set the temperature to around 135°F (57°C) and let them dry for about 8 to 12 hours. The end result should be crispy apple chips that are full of flavor.

When it comes to bananas, you have two options: banana chips or banana leather. To make banana chips, slice the bananas into thin rounds and place them on the dehydrator trays. If you prefer banana leather, puree the bananas in a blender until smooth and spread the mixture onto the dehydrator trays in a thin, even layer. Both options should be dried at a temperature of around 135°F (57°C) for about 6 to 10 hours.

Berries, such as strawberries, blueberries, and raspberries, can be dried as whole fruits or pureed into fruit leathers. For whole berries, simply wash and dry them thoroughly before placing them on the dehydrator trays. Set the temperature to around 135°F (57°C) and let them dry for about 6 to 12 hours, depending on the size of the berries. If you prefer fruit leathers, blend the berries until smooth and spread the mixture onto the dehydrator trays. Dry them at the same temperature for about 6 to 8 hours.

Now that you know how to dehydrate these popular fruits, let's move on to some tips for preserving their natural sweetness and texture. It's important to choose ripe fruits that are at their peak flavor for the best results. Wash them thoroughly and remove any bruised or damaged areas before dehydrating.

One trick to preserve the natural sweetness is to soak the fruits in a solution of lemon juice and water before dehydrating. This not only adds a tangy flavor but also helps prevent browning. You can also sprinkle a little bit of sugar or powdered honey on the fruits before drying to enhance their sweetness.

To maintain the texture of dehydrated fruits, store them in airtight containers or vacuum seal bags. This helps seal in the moisture and prevents them from becoming too dry or crumbly. If you notice any moisture accumulating in the container, simply return the fruits to the dehydrator for a short period to remove any excess moisture.

With these techniques and tips, you'll be able to master the art of dehydrating a variety of fruits. It's a great way to preserve their flavor and enjoy delicious snacks or meals during your outdoor adventures.

Maximizing flavor and nutritional value in dehydrated vegetables

Welcome back! In this section, we will dive into the art of dehydrating vegetables for backpacking and camping adventures. Not only will you learn how to retain the nutrients and flavors of the vegetables, but you will also discover effective techniques to preserve food without sacrificing taste. So let's get started and maximize the flavor and nutritional value in your dehydrated vegetables!

When dehydrating vegetables, it's important to start with fresh produce. Choose vegetables that are at the peak of their ripeness for the best flavor and nutritional content. Wash and thoroughly dry the vegetables before beginning the dehydration process. For leafy greens, remove the stems and cut them into bite-sized pieces. For root vegetables, slice them into thin, even pieces. Uniform slicing ensures even drying and rehydrating later on.

Blanching is a useful technique to enhance the flavor, color, and texture of your dehydrated vegetables. To blanch vegetables, bring a pot of water to a boil and immerse the vegetables for a brief period, typically 1-2 minutes. Immediately transfer the blanched vegetables to an ice bath to stop the cooking process. This step helps to preserve the nutrients and vibrant colors of the vegetables.

Once blanched, it's time to dehydrate the vegetables. Spread them out in a single layer on your dehydrator trays, ensuring enough airflow for even drying. Follow the manufacturer's instructions for temperature and time settings. It's important to fully dehydrate the vegetables to remove all moisture and prevent mold or bacterial growth.

To test if your vegetables are properly dehydrated, pinch a few pieces. They should feel dry and brittle. If there is any moisture left, they need more time in the dehydrator. Once fully dehydrated, allow the vegetables to cool completely before storing them in airtight containers.

Now that you have successfully dehydrated your vegetables, let's move on to rehydration and incorporating them into meals for your outdoor adventures!

Before using dehydrated vegetables in your recipes, they need to be rehydrated. There are a few methods you can use. One option is to add the vegetables to boiling water and allow them to simmer for a few minutes until they become tender. Another method is to soak the vegetables in cold water for a few hours or overnight, depending on the desired texture. This method is particularly useful for preparing vegetables used in cold or raw dishes, such as salads.

Rehydrated vegetables can be incorporated into various meals to add flavor and nutrition. Add them to soups, stews, or casseroles for an extra burst of vegetable goodness. Mix them into pasta dishes, rice bowls, or stir-fries to elevate your camping meals. The possibilities are endless!

Remember, when meal planning for extended adventures, dehydrated vegetables are a lightweight and space-saving option that doesn't compromise on nutrition. They provide a convenient way to pack essential vitamins and minerals into your backpack. So get creative, experiment with different flavors, and enjoy the satisfaction of cooking delicious meals with your dehydrated vegetables!

Creative ways to incorporate dehydrated fruits and vegetables into meals

The art of dehydrating for backpacking and camping opens up a world of possibilities when it comes to creating delicious meals for your outdoor adventures. Whether you're hitting the trails for a weekend backpacking trip or embarking on an extended camping expedition, learning to dehydrate and incorporate dried fruits and vegetables into your meals can enhance the flavor and nutritional value of your dishes while saving weight and space in your backpack.

As you delve into the art of dehydrating, you'll quickly discover the endless innovative recipes and ideas for using dehydrated produce in flavorful dishes. From adding dehydrated bananas to your morning oatmeal or using dried mushrooms to elevate the taste of your campfire risotto, there's no limit to the culinary creations you can dream up. In this subchapter, we'll explore creative ways to incorporate dehydrated fruits and vegetables into your outdoor meals, so get ready to be inspired and motivated to take your backpacking cuisine to the next level.

When it comes to backpacking and camping, the benefits of dried fruits and vegetables go beyond adding variety and nutrition to your meals. Dehydrated produce is lightweight, compact, and has a long shelf life, making it an ideal option for extended adventures. Not only does dehydrating your own fruits and vegetables save you money, but it also allows you to have control over the quality of the ingredients. No more worrying about soggy greens or bruised fruits - with dehydrated produce, you can enjoy fresh-tasting ingredients no matter where your outdoor journey takes you.

So, let's dive into the creative ways you can incorporate dehydrated fruits and vegetables into your meals. From snack bars packed with dried berries and nuts to savory stews brimming with dehydrated vegetables, we'll explore recipes that are sure to tantalize your taste buds and fuel your adventures. Get ready to master the art of meal planning for your outdoor excursions and discover the secrets to rehydrating meals for a satisfying dining experience under the stars.

Chapter 13: DIY Dehydrated Meal Kits

Preparing dehydrated meal kits for convenience on the trail

So you've learned about the benefits of pre-preparing dehydrated meal kits for quick and easy cooking, and you're eager to dive into the world of preparing dehydrated meal kits for convenience on the trail. Well, you're in the right place! In this subchapter, we'll explore the art of dehydrating for backpacking and camping and discover effective techniques to preserve food without sacrificing flavor. Get ready for some mouthwatering meals that are perfect for the outdoors!

When it comes to backpacking and camping, weight and space are precious commodities. That's why it's important to learn how to assemble meal kits that are lightweight, compact, and organized. In this subchapter, we'll delve into the secrets of meal planning for extended adventures and show you how to save weight and space in your backpack without compromising nutrition. Are you ready to unlock the art of meal planning?

As outdoor enthusiasts, we know that the dining experience is just as important as the adventure itself. That's why we'll also reveal the secrets to rehydrating meals for a satisfying dining experience on the trail. So let's get started and master the art of dehydrating and meal planning for your next outdoor excursion!

Customizing meal kits based on dietary preferences and restrictions

When it comes to meal kit preparation, one size does not fit all. Everyone has different dietary needs and preferences, and it's important to take those into account when planning and preparing meals. In this section, we'll explore how you can customize meal kits based on dietary preferences and restrictions.

Whether you follow a specific diet like vegetarian, vegan, or gluten-free, or have certain food allergies or intolerances, there are plenty of options to cater to your needs. You don't have to compromise on taste or nutrition when it comes to meal kits.

One way to customize meal kits is by offering a variety of ingredient options. This allows individuals to choose the ingredients that align with their dietary preferences. For example, if someone follows a vegetarian diet, they can opt for plant-based protein sources like tofu or legumes instead of meat.

Another important aspect is accommodating food allergies and intolerances. By clearly labeling and separating ingredients that may cause allergic reactions, individuals can feel confident and safe while preparing their meals. This includes taking precautions to avoid cross-contamination and providing alternative options where necessary.

It's also essential to consider portion sizes and nutritional balance. Some individuals may have specific caloric or macronutrient requirements, and it's important to provide meal kits that meet those needs. This could involve providing options for individuals with different activity levels or dietary goals.

When it comes to creating versatile meal kits, the key is to cater to different tastes and restrictions. This means offering a wide range of flavors and options that can be customized to suit individual preferences.

One strategy is to provide a variety of seasoning and sauce options. This allows individuals to adjust the flavor profiles of their meals based on their personal preferences. Whether it's a spicy kick or a tangy twist, having a range of options ensures that meal kits can be tailored to individual tastes.

In addition to flavor customization, it's important to offer alternatives for common allergens or dietary restrictions. For example, providing gluten-free pasta options or dairy-free cheese alternatives ensures that individuals with specific requirements can still enjoy delicious meals.

Another aspect to consider is portion flexibility. Some individuals may have smaller or larger appetites, and meal kits should be adaptable to meet those needs. This could involve providing multiple portion sizes or offering add-on options for those who require extra servings.

Lastly, offering meal planning resources and suggestions can help individuals navigate their dietary preferences and restrictions with ease. This could include recipe ideas, meal prepping tips, and guidance on how to create balanced meals that cater to specific dietary needs. By providing these resources, individuals can feel empowered and inspired to explore new flavors and options.

Tips for organizing and packing DIY dehydrated meal kits

Now that we've covered the importance of efficient packing and labeling methods for meal kits, let's delve into some tips specifically for organizing and packing DIY dehydrated meal kits. These tips will help you create mouthwatering meals that are perfect for your outdoor adventures.

Tip #1: Plan your meals in advance:

Before you start packing your dehydrated meals, take some time to plan out your menu for the trip. Consider the number of days you'll be hiking or camping and the number of meals you'll need. This will help you determine the quantity of ingredients required and avoid unnecessary waste.

Tip #2: Use airtight containers:

Invest in quality airtight containers to store your dehydrated meals. Mason jars or vacuum-sealed bags are excellent options as they keep the food fresh and prevent air from getting in. Make sure to label each container with the name of the meal and the date it was prepared.

Tip #3: Separate ingredients:

When packing your dehydrated meal kits, separate the ingredients for each meal into individual containers or bags. This will make it easier to access the required ingredients when preparing your meals outdoors. Consider using small zipper bags or silicone storage containers for easy organization.

Tip #4: Prioritize lightweight and compact packaging:

Since you'll be carrying these meal kits in your backpack, it's essential to prioritize lightweight and compact packaging. Opt for lightweight containers and remove any excess packaging to save space and reduce weight.

Tip #5: Include cooking instructions:

Don't forget to include cooking instructions for each meal kit. Write them down on a small card or sheet of paper and place them inside the container. This way, you'll have a quick reference guide when it's time to rehydrate and cook your meal.

So there you have it, some practical tips for organizing and packing DIY dehydrated meal kits. By following these tips, you'll be well-prepared to create delicious meals that are easy to access and enjoy during your outdoor adventures.

Chapter 14: Hydration for Backpacking and Camping

The importance of staying hydrated during outdoor activities

is essential for anyone engaging in outdoor activities. Whether you're backpacking, camping, or embarking on extended adventures, staying hydrated is key to ensuring your body functions optimally. Not only does proper hydration improve physical performance, but it also helps regulate body temperature, aids in digestion, and supports cognitive function.

Signs of dehydration can be subtle, yet they can have a significant impact on your well-being and outdoor experience. Symptoms such as fatigue, dizziness, dry mouth, and decreased urine output are all indications that you need to replenish your fluids. It's important to understand that dehydration can occur even in cold weather, as the dry air and physical exertion can cause the body to lose moisture. Avoiding dehydration by drinking enough fluids throughout the day can help prevent these symptoms and keep you feeling at your best.

The benefits of proper hydration in the wilderness are numerous. When you're well-hydrated, your body can better regulate its temperature, which is especially important in hot environments where overheating can lead to heat exhaustion or heat stroke. Hydration also supports proper digestion, preventing issues such as constipation or upset stomach that can be common during outdoor activities. Additionally, staying properly hydrated can improve your mental focus and decision-making abilities, keeping you sharp and alert during your adventures.

As you embark on outdoor activities, it's crucial to prioritize staying hydrated. Carry enough water with you and make sure to drink regularly, even if you don't feel thirsty. It's better to err on the side of caution and hydrate consistently rather than waiting until you're already dehydrated. You can also enhance your hydration by consuming electrolyte-rich drinks or adding electrolyte tablets to your water. These help replace minerals lost through sweating and aid in fluid absorption.

Strategies for managing hydration while backpacking and camping

When it comes to backpacking and camping, managing hydration is crucial for your overall well-being and enjoyment of the outdoors. In this section, we will discuss strategies for managing hydration while on the trail, and provide insights on alternative hydration sources and techniques for emergency situations.

Managing hydration is all about establishing a hydration schedule and monitoring your water intake. It is essential to stay hydrated at all times, especially when engaging in physically demanding activities. To do this effectively, you need to plan ahead and make sure you have enough water for the duration of your trip.

One way to establish a hydration schedule is by setting reminders on your phone or watch. This will help you stay on track and remind you when it's time to take a drink. It's essential to listen to your body and drink water even if you don't feel thirsty. Dehydration can creep up on you, and prevention is always better than cure.

In addition to water, there are other alternative hydration sources you can consider, especially in emergency situations. One such source is natural water sources found along the trail, such as streams, rivers, or lakes. However, it is crucial to treat or purify this water before consuming it to prevent the risk of waterborne illnesses. There are many lightweight and compact water treatment options available on the market, so make sure to carry one with you on your backpacking or camping trip.

Another alternative hydration technique is using electrolyte tablets or powders. These can be added to your water to replenish essential minerals lost through sweat. Electrolyte drinks can help you stay hydrated and energized during strenuous activities, especially in hot weather conditions.

When it comes to camping, conserving water is essential, especially if you have limited access to fresh water sources. One strategy for conserving water is using a portable camp shower system. These systems allow you to take quick and efficient showers while minimizing water usage.

Another technique for managing hydration while camping is to incorporate foods with high water content into your meals. Fruits and vegetables, such as watermelon, cucumber, and lettuce, are excellent options that can help keep you hydrated. These foods not only provide hydration but also essential nutrients for your adventure.

In conclusion, managing hydration while backpacking and camping is vital for your overall well-being. By establishing a hydration schedule, monitoring your water intake, and considering alternative hydration sources and techniques, you can ensure that you stay hydrated and enjoy your outdoor adventures to the fullest.

Incorporating hydration into meal planning for outdoor adventures

Now that you have learned the essentials of dehydrating for backpacking and camping, it's time to take your meal planning to the next level. In this section, we will dive into the art of incorporating hydration into your outdoor adventures.

When venturing into the great outdoors, it's crucial to prioritize hydration. Dehydration can lead to fatigue, decreased performance, and even more serious health issues. To avoid this, we need to focus on consuming foods and beverages that enhance hydration while planning our meals for extended adventures.

Let's explore some hydration-enhancing foods and beverages that you can include in your dehydrated meal plan:

- Watermelon: This juicy fruit is not only delicious, but it also has a high water content, making it an excellent choice for staying hydrated.
- Cucumbers: With their refreshing crunch, cucumbers are a great addition to your dehydrated meals. They contain about 95% water and provide essential electrolytes like potassium.
- Coconut water: Packed with natural electrolytes, coconut water is a fantastic hydrating beverage to include in your outdoor meal plan.
- Oranges: These citrus fruits are not only refreshing but are also rich in water content and packed with vitamin C.
- Broths or soups: Adding dehydrated broths or soups to your meals can provide both hydration and essential nutrients.

Now that you have some ideas for hydration-enhancing foods and beverages, let's move on to some tips that will help you prevent dehydration and optimize your hydration strategy:

- Drink water frequently: Make it a habit to take small sips of water throughout the day, even if you don't feel thirsty. This will help prevent dehydration.
- Monitor your urine color: One of the easiest ways to check your hydration status is by observing the color of your urine. Aim for a pale yellow color, indicating adequate hydration.
- Use electrolyte supplements: Especially during intense outdoor activities, electrolyte supplements can help replenish the salts and minerals lost through sweat.
- Limit caffeine and alcohol intake: Both caffeine and alcohol can contribute to dehydration, so it's best to minimize their consumption during your outdoor adventures.
- Plan your water sources: Research the availability of water sources along your route and plan accordingly. Carry enough water and consider options for filtration or purification.

By incorporating these tips into your meal planning and hydration strategy, you'll be well-prepared to stay hydrated and energized during your outdoor adventures.

Remember, hydration plays a crucial role in maintaining your performance and overall well-being. Don't overlook it as you plan your meals for extended backpacking and camping trips. With a little extra attention to hydration, you can enjoy a satisfying dining experience and make the most of your time in nature.

Chapter 15: Advanced Dehydrating Techniques

Exploring complex recipes and meal ideas for experienced campers

In the previous chapter, we explored the world of challenging and innovative dehydrated meal options for outdoor gourmets. Now, it's time to take it up a notch and delve into advanced techniques and ingredients that will elevate your outdoor dining experiences. Whether you're an experienced camper or just looking to up your game in the great outdoors, this subchapter is packed with exciting recipes and meal ideas that will leave your taste buds craving for more.

When it comes to outdoor cooking, complexity doesn't have to be a hindrance. In fact, it can be a gateway to a whole new level of culinary adventure. This section will introduce you to a range of complex recipes and meal ideas that are perfect for experienced campers like yourself. From multi-course feasts to fusion dishes that blend different cuisines, these recipes will push the boundaries of what you thought was possible in outdoor cooking.

Imagine savoring a mouthwatering three-course meal under the stars, starting with an appetizer of crispy kale chips seasoned with a blend of exotic spices. For the main course, indulge in a tender and succulent Moroccan-style lamb tagine, slow-cooked to perfection using traditional spices and preserved lemons. And for dessert, treat yourself to a warm and gooey chocolate lava cake, cooked in a Dutch oven and served with a dollop of homemade vanilla bean ice cream.

This subchapter will guide you through the process of creating these culinary masterpieces step by step, providing detailed instructions and tips to ensure your success. You'll learn about the different techniques and ingredients that will take your outdoor cooking to the next level, from sous vide cooking to using unique herbs and spices. Our goal is to inspire you to think outside the box and create unforgettable dining experiences in the wilderness.

But it's not just about the recipes. In this section, we'll also explore the art of meal planning for extended adventures. We'll show you how to plan your meals in advance, taking into consideration factors such as nutritional balance, weight savings, and storage space. You'll discover clever tips and tricks for packing your backpack efficiently, so you can enjoy delicious and nourishing meals on even the most demanding outdoor adventures.

Furthermore, we'll unlock the secrets to rehydrating meals for a satisfying dining experience. Dehydrated meals are a staple for backpackers and campers, but often they can lack flavor and texture. We'll share tips and techniques for rehydrating meals to perfection, ensuring that every bite is packed with flavor and satisfaction. From proper hydration times to creative additions that enhance the taste, you'll become a pro at transforming dehydrated ingredients into culinary delights.

So, get ready to take your outdoor cooking skills to new heights. Get inspired by complex recipes, master the art of meal planning, and become a rehydration expert. With this knowledge and these techniques, you'll never settle for ordinary campsite meals again. Your taste buds and fellow campers will thank you!

Innovative dehydrating methods for unique and gourmet outdoor meals

When it comes to dehydrating meals for outdoor adventures, there are plenty of innovative methods you can use to create unique and gourmet dishes. In this subchapter, we'll dive into some of these techniques and explore how they can elevate your camping and backpacking experience.

Innovative dehydrating methods can help you create meals that are not only lightweight and easy to pack, but also bursting with flavor and texture. One such technique is sous vide dehydration, which involves cooking food in a vacuum-sealed bag at a precise low temperature in a water bath. This method allows for maximum flavor retention and results in tender and succulent meals.

Another technique you can experiment with is flash freezing. By rapidly freezing food at extremely low temperatures, you can preserve its natural flavors and textures. Flash-frozen meals can be easily rehydrated on the trail, making them a convenient option for quick and satisfying meals.

By pushing the boundaries of flavor and texture in dehydrated meals, you can create gourmet dishes that will impress even the most discerning outdoor food enthusiasts. Think outside the box and explore unconventional combinations of ingredients. For example, you could try dehydrating fruits like mango and pairing them with savory ingredients like bacon for a sweet and salty treat.

When it comes to meal planning for extended adventures, effective food preservation techniques are essential. Dehydrating meals allows you to save weight and space in your backpack without compromising on nutrition. With the right planning, you can ensure that you have delicious and nourishing meals at your fingertips throughout your outdoor journey.

Rehydrating meals is an art in itself. It's important to find the right balance of water and time to bring your dehydrated meals back to life. Experiment with different rehydration methods and ratios to achieve the perfect texture and taste. Whether you're rehydrating a hearty stew or a flavorful pasta dish, the key is to allow the ingredients to fully absorb the water and regain their original flavors and textures.

So, get ready to take your outdoor cooking skills to the next level. With innovative dehydrating methods and a willingness to experiment, you'll be able to create mouthwatering meals that are perfect for the outdoors. Happy cooking!

Don't miss out!

Visit the website below and you can sign up to receive emails whenever DANA MCCARTHY publishes a new book. There's no charge and no obligation.

https://books2read.com/r/B-A-ZEUDB-LDCXC

BOOKS2READ

Connecting independent readers to independent writers.

Did you love *Dehydrating Food - Dehydrating For Backpacking And Camping*? Then you should read *Beginners Guide To Dehydrating Food*[1] by DANA MCCARTHY!

The Beginners Guide To Dehydrating Food

If you're interested in learning how to preserve and make delicious, nutritious snacks, then "The Beginners Guide To Dehydrating Food" is the perfect resource for you. This comprehensive guide takes you through everything you need to know about dehydrating food, from the benefits to choosing the right tools and equipment. Dive into understanding which fruits and vegetables are best for dehydration and learn tricks for successful dehydration. Discover how to create tasty dehydrated fruits, such as apples, bananas, and berries, as well as making fruit leathers and snacks. Explore the world of dehydrated vegetables,

---

1. https://books2read.com/u/balBwa

2. https://books2read.com/u/balBwa

including tomatoes, peppers, and carrots, and learn how to make vegetable chips and powders. Pick up tips on dehydrating herbs and spices, as well as meats and jerky. Get expert advice on proper storage methods for your dehydrated food and learn how to incorporate them into your favorite recipes. Troubleshooting common issues, planning meals, and trying out advanced techniques and recipes are also covered. Whether you're a beginner or looking to expand your dehydrating skills, this guide will equip you with the knowledge and inspiration to get started.

Also by DANA MCCARTHY

Beginners Guide To Dehydrating Food
Dehydrating Food - Dehydrating For Backpacking And Camping